Stitched Together

STORIES FOR THE QUILTER'S SOUL

—— VOLUME 3 ——

MISSOURI STAR
—— QUILT CO. ——

Edited by Katie Mifsud and Nichole Spravzoff
Designed by Ally Simmons
Cover photo by BPD Studios

Table of Contents

Quilters are a special breed. Always generous, you teach each other, inspire one another, and share ideas, chocolate, and stories. My goodness, I love the stories! The things we have heard from you as you've visited us or written to us have changed the way we see the world, and we never cease to be amazed by your incredible stories of generosity, heritage, and hope.

Ever since we had a story contest for National Quilting Month in March 2014, which we repeated in 2015, we have opened our mailbox and our hearts to your stories and we have been richly rewarded! Every week we receive more stories of the experiences that have brought you to quilting, some heartbreaking, some heartwarming, and there are a few have made us laugh out loud.

Collecting these stories has become a particularly special part of what we do here. We laugh and cry along with you as we read about the stories behind your quilts and we realize more than ever that we are all a part of a worldwide quilting family.

Thank you for sharing your stories and for being part of our family.

Jenny

P.S. If you have a story you'd like to share, send it on over to stories@missouriquiltco.com, and watch for more stories every Tuesday at missouriquiltco.com/shop/dailydeal.

Second Chances

by **DEBBIE ROBERTS**
Crossville, Tennessee

I had been a single mother to two wonderful kids for eleven years when I met Joel. He asked me to marry him after we had known each other for only three days! Six weeks later, Joel and I married and we moved from Florida to Kansas City, Missouri, and began a whole new life. For the first time in my adult life I had a wee bit of breathing room financially and signed up for a quilting class. What a joy to learn another skill to add to a lifetime of sewing! The first quilt I made was for my fourteen-year-old son, Jarrad.

The pattern was called "Around the Twist" and had creamy snowball blocks in between navy strips. In class we learned how to draw around the templates onto the fabric, one by one, cut the fabric out, and hand stitch all the pieces together. Yes, we hand stitched them together! Our teacher wanted us to learn how to quilt the way our ancestors did and I relished every moment working on that quilt. When the quilt was completed, I simply tied the quilt sandwich together with bright red embroidery thread in the center of each cream block, since I had no idea

how to hand quilt at that time. That was the beginning of my love affair with quilting.

After high school, Jarrad joined the U.S. Navy and took the quilt with him on the ship to remind him of home. That poor quilt got tossed in the ship's laundry more than once over four years at sea and even saw a bit of bleach, I'm afraid.

Almost thirty years have gone by and I now make quilts for clients. I think my skills have improved a little since that first class all those years ago. My husband and I recently retired to a farm in Tennessee. Last year was our first Christmas on the farm and we were looking forward to a sweet time celebrating the holiday. Two days before Christmas, on my birthday, Jarrad called and said, "Happy Birthday, Mom. I've got lymphoma."

Our world turned upside down with that call. It was decided that my husband would stay on the farm with our youngest son while I drove, alone and crying on Christmas Day, to reach Jarrad in Florida. The day after Christmas was scary as tests were done, a port was installed in Jarrad's chest to receive medicine, and chemo began. At his first chemo session he was cold and the sweet nurses covered him up with warm flannel blankets. I could do nothing but watch and soothe him with words and prayer. Wasn't there something else I could do?

And then I remembered. Two years earlier, I had "stolen" that first ragged quilt (with my daughter-in-law's approval) with the thought that I'd repair it one day and give it back to Jarrad. I made a quick phone call to Joel back in Tennessee and told him exactly where the quilt was in my studio and asked him to please ship it to me right away. I just had to have something to work on with my hands while we went through this ordeal together. It arrived a few days later and so began the process of hand stitching once again—only this time it was to repair the gaping seams that had torn open with all the rough handling in the Navy's laundry. Embroidery helped to cover some areas that were almost beyond repair. Pinning the flopping quilt sandwich back together helped to make the worn quilt look much better. My first quilt teacher must have instructed us to save the fabric left over from the quilt as I had a little plastic bag with the original fabric still all together! It really came in handy doing the repairs and I even had enough to replace the original binding, which now was nothing more than threads clinging to the quilt edge.

I didn't get the quilt done while in Florida, but thinking about Jarrad sitting in that chair getting chemo and shivering spurred me on to stitch faster and faster. A couple weeks later, when I gave the quilt to Jarrad, it had a proper label on it, detailing its long journey and who it was made for. Jarrad was so happy to have his quilt back and snuggled under it for many hours over the six courses of chemo he received. He says the quilt helped him feel comforted, feeling as if I was there with him through the quilt.

We are happy to report that Jarrad is done with chemo and has had clean PET scans since completing his therapy in May. Even though I couldn't be with him for all those miserable months of chemo, he says a part of me was always there, holding him ... in the folds of a quilt.

Insist On Celebrating

by **JEANNE ELMES**
Morgantown, West Virginia

It's been several years now since I made my first quilt. I was a member of Women Across Cultures in the university town of Morgantown, West Virginia, and a friend of mine from Belgium suggested that we should all teach each other a skill. Anneke taught us (well, dragged some of us through) making a quilted pillow cover, piecing and quilting by hand, of course. My skills did not include precision anything, so I was made to stop, rip, restitch, and try again at every step. Yes, I still have that pillow. And then I had a wild idea, because I tend to try new things without thinking of the impossibilities, but once I'm in, I'm in.

My parents' fiftieth anniversary was on the horizon, and my siblings and I decided to throw a surprise party for them. I had decided, purely on the strength of my quilted pillow success, that I would make them a full size signature quilt with all, or most, of their friends' signatures from their many years and places. It was a gigantic task!

Somehow I managed to sneakily gather the names and addresses of their friends from Minnesota, Colorado, and Arizona—including family, friends from work, and all others that I could think of. I pieced twelve by twelve Irish Chain blocks, admittedly with inexpensive fabric (because of affordability and ignorance) and mailed each block, along with a fabric pen, to all of these people. Many friends then gathered a few more signatures of people they knew should be included. They, in turn, were delighted to be included in the secret project and helped from afar. I'd asked in an accompanying letter to please return the blocks by a certain date so I could sew them all together and begin hand quilting, but don't worry, I had not pieced the blocks by hand!

Long story short, the memory quilt full of signatures came together and I hand quilted my first ever quilt in time to wrap it up and put it in the car for the trek across the country with my husband and four children.

At the huge surprise anniversary party, Mom and Dad were duly surprised, humbled by the gathering, a little embarrassed by all the attention (good Midwestern upbringing here), and moved to tears by the friendships surrounding them.

I then grabbed the microphone and said that I had a gift for them. As my mom opened the package, she was saying something like, "Oh, Jeanne, you know I don't need anything …" Then I watched her face turn slowly to surprise, then glistening tears, as she realized what she

was looking at. Watching her response affirmed my "just do it" way of living life.

Mom was so moved by how much of their history was collected together just with the signatures on the quilt and the way it came together that she easily convinced Dad that they should get in their motorhome and take a roadtrip to add a few more signatures that I had not gathered. Pen, quilt, and camera in hand, they traveled back to Arizona and Colorado, visiting friends, telling the story, and enjoying time with old friends.

A few months after that journey, Mom was gone ... congestive heart failure. But she and Dad had done a wonderful thing together, finding and being grateful for friends and experiences of their life together.

That was in 1992 and 1993. The quilt has been back with me for several years now and its story continues. Three of our four children have married, with the fourth to marry next summer. The "family rag" goes along to the weddings and collects signatures of the new family around the block that the couples have chosen and "signed in on" at their engagements.

The latest wedding was in May 2015. I took the quilt along to a picnic the day after where we continued to celebrate with new family and old friends. That's where the quilt came out to have new family "sign in." As it happened, one of our grandchildren was worn out and needed to lie down for a bit, so I ran to the car, retrieved the quilt, and made a nest for him on the ground. His dad said, "Oh, Jeanne, you don't want to put that on the ground do you? Kilian will be fine without it." But I replied, "Oh, no, Michael, it's fine. This is what it is for." With smiles all around, four year old Kilian had a brief, restorative nap.

The old family quilt—faded, with a wonderful mess of signatures—always reminds me of the beauty of life. It's a tangible reminder to love each other and insist on celebrating the uniqueness all around, in between, and among us.

The Little Flyers Quilt

by **STAR NOVAK**
Lecompton, Kansas

I work in the aviation world, and have done so for many years. This past summer my guy was spraying corn in Iowa; he's an aerial applicator, a.k.a. crop-duster. I stumbled across the MSQC website and immediately found the Riley Blake "Little Flyers" 5″ squares. I had to have it and bought it immediately, not even knowing what in the world to do with it. My friend Jennifer at work suggested a baby stroller-sized quilt for my first project, which seemed fitting enough since my first granddaughter was just a couple of months old. After work one evening, Jennifer showed me how easy it was to make a raggy-edge quilt. I was so excited I spilled the beans to my daughter, who did not share my aviation-related enthusiasm. Crestfallen, I told Jennifer that this project "just wouldn't fly," and with her help, I laid out a quilt for her baby girl in cute colors and patterns, and completed it quickly.

But my first quilt project with the "Little Flyers" fabric kept calling my name. I decided to make the quilt anyway and I chose a fun lime green and a grey polka dot fabric to compliment the prints. I completed the quilt that weekend and it turned out great! I proudly showed it off at

work on Monday, and the ladies all loved it. I was so very proud of myself and my accomplishment.

I decided that I would take my "Little Flyers" quilt to our State Agriculture Aviators' conference, which was just a few weeks away, to see if it could be auctioned off to benefit our Association. I showed up at the convention with my quilt neatly folded and tied with a bright yellow bow just to hear the most devastating news: a dear friend of mine in the Association had been diagnosed with cancer.

I placed my quilt in the auction, and another friend suggested that we donate the proceeds of the quilt to our friend. I wholeheartedly agreed, and the auctioneer asked me to say a few words about my quilt. It was a challenge to keep my composure as I walked the quilt around to show the prospective bidders; I could hardly see through tear-filled eyes. The

bidding started off briskly and I was amazed that this crowd of mostly gentlemen, who usually zero in on the rifles and GPS products, would be so interested in my little quilt. Soon the bidding was at $5,000 and the quilt was sold. I could hardly believe my ears. It had brought in more money than anything else at the auction!

The secretary whispered in my ear that the purchaser had very generously donated the quilt back to the Association and asked if I would I like to resell it. I numbly nodded yes, voiced my thanks into the auctioneer's mic, and started my parade again. The quilt was sold again ... and again and again, with each purchaser donating the quilt back to the Association. The amount raised at the auction from my humble, little, first-ever baby stroller "Little Flyers" quilt was over $21,000 for our friend and her family! I was stunned, and so very thankful. My oh my how proud I was to be standing in that room holding that quilt! The feeling of love and support from the crowd was overwhelming. It was all a blur to me to be interviewed by our featured speaker at the convention for his national radio show, and to have photos taken with the quilt purchasers. The giving continued as friends, vendors, and people I didn't even know placed money in my hand and nodded at me with heartfelt smiles. Our check total wound up to be over $22,500 in the end.

My friend who has cancer lives in southwestern Kansas and we decided to fly out the following weekend to give her the check in person, since she was not able to go to the convention this year. We arranged for several other couples to fly in as well to surprise her. It was a beautiful fall day for our trip, and we made it in around two hours from Eastern Kansas, in our Cessna 175. With several other Association ladies around me, I gave our friend the quilt and the check. Understandably, there were plenty of tears and hugs, with my quilt in the center of it all. We laughed together at the sayings on the fabric like "I must fly, my people need me," and the cute airplane graphics. It was a wonderful afternoon.

My friend didn't put the quilt down all day, preferring to hold on to it tightly. All too soon, it was getting late, and time for us to head back to Topeka. One by one our airplane friends took off, flew over the hangar and buzzed the runway. We took off last, buzzed the runway, and as I looked back, I could see my quilt still held tightly in my friend's arms as she energetically waved at me. My guy pulled the Cessna hard into a traditional ag pilot's turn. I pressed my face into the copilot's side glass to hide my tears. I watched my friend standing by the runway getting smaller and smaller in the distance, but feeling the love and support stitched into my quilt burning brighter and brighter.

What Might Have Been

by **JODY BOEST**
Houston, Texas

S everal years ago, when I was helping my ninety-year-old mother move out of her house and into a smaller place, I found several paper bags filled with appliquéd quilt squares. Some were in perfect condition, some were only half-finished, and some were stained with age and moth-eaten. When I asked my mom about them, this is the story she told:

My great-grandmother, Minnie Mae, was the daughter of a Methodist minister in a small town in rural Pennsylvania. As a young woman, she became engaged to a local boy who was preparing to study medicine. Her future mother-in-law was a quilter and started making a quilt for the happy couple, as a wedding gift. Then, when a handsome drifter arrived in town, he took one look at Minnie Mae and swept her off her feet. The wedding was off, Minnie Mae was in love with someone else, and the future mother-in-law was furious! To show her anger, she brought all the unassembled quilt squares to Minnie Mae and threw them on the ground at her feet. Minnie

Mae saved the squares in paper bags and they were passed down through the generations.

I was fascinated by this story and took the squares to a local quilter who confirmed that the quilt squares were indeed made from old fabric, pre-1900's. So I purchased some Civil War reproduction fabric at my local quilt shop and started assembling the quilt into a wall hanging, which I presented to my sister, the family genealogist.

I'd like to say that the story of Minnie Mae had a happy ending, but the handsome drifter, my great-grandfather, ended up abandoning Minnie Mae and their two children several years later. The jilted fiancée went on to become a very prominent and wealthy doctor. Sigh ... would life have been different for her if those original quilt squares had been given as a wedding gift? No one will ever know!

Who I Come From

by **JOYCE GERBER BLUE**
Cheyenne, Wyoming

My grandfather, George Howard Bogue, came to Wyoming from Pennsylvania as a five-year-old boy. His mother died and his father put him and his siblings in an orphanage for a while, then moved them west in a covered wagon. George learned to sew by making his and his siblings' clothes. He stayed with his sister long after she was married and had children to help raise them. When the children were old enough to go to high school, he moved to town so they would have a place to live while they attended school. There he met a pretty young school teacher who won his heart. Her name was Joyce Edith Stanton and she was from Coal Creek, around the Sundance area. They married and had eight kids, one of which was my mother.

They worked hard to raise these children through the Depression and a World War. Living in a one-bedroom house they raised gardens, canned, and did everything they could to survive. George sheared sheep, worked on roads, and then went to work for the U.S. Post Office. He eventually retired and then opened a saw filing business in an outbuilding on their

property. He did this for years then had to retire from that occupation due to his health. He needed something to do, so he fell back on the one thing that kept his family going so many years before: sewing. He had a cabinet by his chair in which he kept his supplies. He would cut out pieces of fabric on a piece of wood on his lap and stack them ever so nicely and thread needle after needle and put them in several pincushions with the thread hanging down. It never got tangled. As a child I would watch him sew those tiny pieces together and marvel at what his fingers could produce. It was amazing to me.

He made hundreds of quilt tops and gave them away to family members and he also donated some quilts to charities. I got one on my wedding day and a few later on when I would stop to visit with my husband and two daughters.

Grandpa wanted to do something special for his bride of fifty years, so he made her a quilt with one-inch blocks. It was multicolored and he had it hand quilted. It was beautiful. As you could imagine, it was Grandma's favorite quilt. She had it on her bed for years, even after Grandpa passed away. My brother came to visit with his wife one day and Grandma, on a whim, took the quilt off her bed and gave it to them. What a treasure that was. My brother died four years ago and his wife gave it to his twin and his wife. They decided that since I was a quilter, I should have it. So now it is on my antique bed so I can see it every day and remember who I come from.

The Gift of Warmth

by **JENNIFER ZAMPOGNA**
Cheyenne, Wyoming

Six years ago my family was involved in a double-fatality accident. I lost my husband. He was my best friend, confidant, and the father of my children. There was extensive damage to my leg in the accident as well and the surgeries and physical therapy that followed were daunting at best. I spent a month in the hospital and, in that time, each of my family members received a small quilt. I didn't think much more of them than, "That was very nice."

As the dust settled, I gathered what was left of my life and tried to make heads or tails of what the new normal was going to be. I was sitting in my room when the quilt that had been given to my husband while on life support caught my eye. I began to think about the warmth that the quilt had given him while I couldn't, like a constant hug. I found myself wandering to each of my kids' rooms and finding their brightly colored quilts. Remembering the kids with them and gazing at the cheerful colors made me realize that these quilts were more than just nice gifts.

Wanting to give others the gift of warmth and brightness, I found myself enrolling in a quilt class at a local shop, Quilted Corner, and I found joy again. Each stitch, new pattern, and completed quilt slowly brought me out of the very dark place where I had been. Now when I give a quilt it's more than thread and cloth. It's a hug when I am not there to give one and a softly whispered "I love you."

Noah Afloat

by **PAULA DIGGLE**
London, United Kingdom

A few years ago, my boss came over to my desk during lunch break and asked if I had a baby quilt she could take when she visited her niece in Cairo, Egypt, that Christmas, just a few days away. By good fortune I did have one, a bright Ohio Star quilt using fabrics with a Noah's Ark theme. Not a work of art, but easy on the eye, I called the quilt "Noah Afloat." My boss loved it. So did the young mum. I was happy it had all worked out and I gave it no further thought.

It must have been the following summer that my boss came over to me to talk quilts on our lunch break again. She told me of how her niece had turned up on her parents' doorstep unannounced, just a few days before. Her niece had her son with her and not much else. She did have the quilt though. It seems her possessive husband had made her life in Egypt a misery, never letting her go out of the house, but, she had managed to escape with the help of a Western friend. She didn't take much with her, but she couldn't leave the quilt.

By the end of this story my boss and I were fighting back the tears. I don't quite know how I got through the afternoon. I share this because I have come to believe that there is power in a quilt. That quilt hadn't been made for that particular little boy, but it still comforted him, and that's truly something.

Noah Afloat indeed.

Something More Precious

by **RAMONA BACHMANN**
Raanana, Israel

I was born in India in a Jewish community consisting of Jews from Baghdad, Persia, Ceylon (today called Sri Lanka), and a community called Bnei Israel (Children of Israel) who lived there for many generations. We had a big, beautiful synagogue attended by nearly all.

When some kind of happy occasion occurred like marriage, birth, or someone felt they were fortunate in some special way, the family would contribute something to beautify the synagogue.

The Persians, mostly carpet merchants, were the most well off and would give a big velvet and gold curtain to cover the ark where the Torah scrolls were kept so everyone could see how prestigious it was! The Iraqi Jews from Baghdad could afford something more modest in cotton and embroidery, but each family would give what they could and it was clear who had more and who less.

In the community was a very, very old lady. I was only about ten years of age and in my eyes she looked a hundred years old! She was very poor and lived in a small dark room where she used to repair clothes or sew small skull caps (yarmulkes) for the men to wear on their heads while praying. As she sewed, she collected the tiniest leftover pieces of fabric. By hand sewing them all together, she made a huge curtain; I would say it was a king-size cover. She presented it to the person responsible for the synagogue, who did not want to hurt her feelings, and that person decided to hang it in front of the Torah Ark.

Anyone who saw it said "Oh poor lady. She cannot afford to give something more precious." But, and here comes my personal love for patchwork and quilting, when I saw this work of thousands of hand-pieced fabric bits displayed, I was so enlightened. I admired it thinking how beautiful it appeared and what a tremendous effort it must have been to make it. Since then, whenever I see small pieces of fabric, I think of that immense work, and I cannot get myself to throw away even the smallest piece of fabric.

Today I am seventy three years old and I have sewn hundreds of patchwork projects, but what I would not give to see that fantastic work again!

A Beautiful Thread

***

by **CHERYL SKILES**
Middletown, California

My story is a bittersweet one. On September 12, 2015, I spent the day out of the area celebrating my oldest daughter Hannah's birthday. My daughter, Heidi, and granddaughter, Penelope, and I came home to overwhelming wind, smoke, and fire cresting over the mountain ridge behind our house. We had less than one hour to grab our things, get the big dogs out, and evacuate. I was one of those who, in my panic, had tunnel vision and didn't have the time or the foresight to grab many special things, including some precious quilts. Afterward, I woke up many nights, mourning the loss of a favorite folk-style felted wool quilt I had made over ten years ago and a special quilt my sister Karen and I had made together for my fiftieth birthday. But God went ahead of me and I found a beautiful unfinished quilt in my sewing studio, which was the only building left standing, out of the fire's devastating path.

This wind-driven Valley Fire destroyed over 1,200 homes and several lives in just eight short hours. Several weeks after the fire, my sister and

I went to a local quilt show and met a couple of ladies who had traveled many hours and had coordinated some notions and fabrics for me and other victims to pick out in order to start up our stashes again. Several weeks after that, I was invited to come look through some quilts many people donated to the fire victims. I had a lovely pink and green guest bedroom and I decided I would repeat that color theme in my new house. When I went to Kerry's quilt shop, I picked out a lovely pink and green quilt donated just for my bedroom! Then, a few weeks later, I was invited to a lovely tea at her quilt shop and was given a quilt made up of hearts donated from people as far as Hawaii and Kansas. These blocks were sent to her quilt shop and many ladies donated their time to assemble and quilt them for us who had lost so much. Our local quilting community has been like a beautiful thread woven through my heart as I begin to patch up and rebuild my life.

Helen's Garden

by **JANE METZGER**
Kansas City, Missouri

My mom, Helen, has always been my hero and I have always proudly told anyone that I am a mama's girl. Almost fifty years ago, my mother taught me how to use a sewing machine. She could sew, but never enjoyed it as a creative outlet. To her it was more as a means to an end. Instead, my mom embraced gardening, specifically flower gardening. She spent countless hours planting and tending her garden; she never met a flower that she felt was unworthy. To Mom, each flower had a merriment of its own. She loved color and organized chaos.

I, however, embraced the joy of sewing. I especially love how quilting takes ideas and colors and transforms them. Patterns and a little spirit and can turn even the most ordinary fabric into something beautifully organized and useful.

Two years ago, my mother became ill and I traveled hundreds of miles from my home to take care of her. My mom was sick and she needed me. The gardens and the sewing could wait.

About a year after my mom died, I was with some friends exploring

a wonderful store not far from our home called Missouri Star Quilt

Company. MSQC has a Daily Deal each day and when we were there, it

was a charm pack called Helen's Garden. Now, while this is a beautiful

grouping of prints, I probably would not have selected it on my own,

based solely on its appearance. It's just not my style, I guess. But the

name: Helen's Garden, well that got me. How could I pass that little

charm pack up? So I bought one and brought it home. It sat for close to

a year on my sewing table, but as unique and pretty as it was, it never

called to me to be made into a quilt.

Then one day I picked up a quilting book by Sue Pfau. In that book was a gorgeous coin quilt she had titled Garden Trellis. This was it! This was the quilt the little Helen's Garden charm pack needed! I went online and ordered additional charm packs so I could start my tribute quilt. It went together quickly and beautifully. It's colorful and cheerful and random and yet still organized. Instead of using traditional batting, I placed one of my Mom's lightweight blankets that she always referred to as a "sheet blanket" inside the quilt. My daughter thinks the quilt just looks happy.

I will live the rest of my life missing my mom. She was truly one of my heroes and she taught me to see beauty and to organize randomness to the point where it was unique and cheerful. So the Helen's Garden charm pack became a happy little garden trellis quilt. To top it off, the title of the book containing the pattern was Quilts from Sweet Jane. My name is Jane.

Sometimes you just feel like maybe the universe puts little things together for you.

Make New Friends But Keep the Old

by **JACOBA GELDERMAN**
Waterdown, Ontario

When I was a little girl, we lived up north in Ontario, Canada, in a very small town called Matheson. Due to my father's poor health, we moved from the farm to a larger town in Southern Ontario called Fergus when I was fourteen. When we left Matheson, we were told by my parents that we were now starting a new life and we would not be able to write to our friends in Matheson because we should put this time behind us. I had a girlfriend named Nellie who was a year older than me and we totally lost contact with each other as a result.

I started quilting at around the age of forty five and of course I was addicted immediately. Since I had sewn all my life, I was already in love with fabrics and putting things together. As an adult, I moved to the Waterdown, Ontario, area and have lived all my married life here. Two years ago I joined a wonderful group of ladies from our area churches and we meet every other Thursday at one of our homes. In London,

Ontario, about two hours from where we meet, there is another group of similar ladies who meet every Tuesday. We also get together once a year to enjoy a day of Show and Tell, lunch, and fellowship.

At my first quilting group, I met one of the ladies from the London group and we chatted quite a while. We exchanged emails because we both love Chinese tea and she could get it straight from China. Her name was Nellie. We emailed each other for almost a year, mostly about quilting and tea. Then one day I was at one of my Thursday groups and somehow her name came up. Someone else from the group asked another lady if she knew who Nellie was. The other lady said: "Nellie VanderVegte?" and my heart completely stopped! I couldn't believe that it was "my" Nellie!

As soon as I got home, I emailed her right away and asked her if she was the Nellie from Matheson and told her how shocked I was that I hadn't realized who she was. She emailed me right back and asked me if I was Coby Post, her friend from childhood. Both of us had different last names, and I had also reverted back to my baptism name when I was a teen. It had been close to fifty years since we had completely lost touch. Once we found each other again through our love for quilting, there was so much to talk about! We met again that weekend and have been as close as sisters ever since. We talk or text many times a week and we have so much in common from our faith, to our grown children (five each), to quilting. I'm so grateful that my love of quilting helped me rediscover the love of a great friend!

Made by Daddy and Me

✶

by **SANDI KING**
Fayetteville, Tennessee

Let me start this by saying that my mother did not want me. I say this simply, not to garner any sympathy; it is just a fact of life that I knew by instinct at a very early age. Therefore, my daddy became the most important person in the whole world to me.

He taught me everything I needed to know in life, including when I was nine and decided I wanted to learn how to sew. Let me start by saying that my father was a big Italian man with a neck as thick as a tree trunk and hands the size of dinner plates. He was a building contractor and he said if he could read a blueprint, we could surely read a pattern together. So off we went to the fabric store where we bought enough fabric to clothe every child born that year and a shiny, brand new sewing machine. Of course we also had to get just about every gadget on the sewing wall that said, "You need me."

We made a dress. I wore it to church that very Sunday and I was so proud I could burst. Okay, it probably wasn't as beautiful as I remember it, but my daddy and I made it and to me it was gorgeous. About a year later I decided it was time for us to learn how to quilt. I can still see his huge hands trying to hold those little needles and make tiny stitches. I still have that quilt, even though my daddy has been gone since 1984. My quilts now are more perfected and I sell them for a profit, but the most valuable quilt I own is the one I have hanging on the quilt rack that my daddy and I made. I'll never forget the sacrifices he made, the time he spent, and the love he gave, all just for me.

When the Perfect Person Comes Along

by **BONNIE SKINNER**
Dyersburg, Tennessee

I have been quilting and sewing for over fifty years. I make many quilt tops and when I can afford it, a special top will make its way to the quilter. Last year I completed a One Block Wonder quilt in beautiful gold, black, cream, and pink fabric. My husband was impressed and said that it would have to go to someone very special. I usually don't have anyone in mind when I make a quilt, so they just hang around the quilt room until the perfect person comes along.

Recently, my husband had to have triple bypass heart surgery. He spent eight days in the hospital and was released on a Friday. By that evening, he wasn't feeling too good, so I called Tina, a good friend and neighbor who is a nurse, to come over and check his blood pressure. Unfortunately, his pressure was bottoming out, and we called for an ambulance to take him back to the hospital. After four more days of medication adjustments he was released again.

Thankfully, he is much better now and we are so grateful for Tina, our wonderful neighbor who jumped out of bed and came over to help in her pajamas! She saved my husband's life. And, that "special person" my husband talked about? You guessed it! That beautiful quilt found its person and new home! When I presented her with the quilt she cried, and I cried, but they were tears of joy and love!

Why Not Me?

by **LIN KASSHA**
Vallejo, California

In 1995 I was hit by a drunk driver and I lost all but about 10% of my vision. My left eye is totally blind. I was depressed, sad, and angry. Two things ate away at me: the first was not being able to sew or quilt, which was my hobby and love for the last thirty years, and the second was not being able to drive to the fabric store.

Last year I was surfing the internet on my voice controlled computer and came across the Missouri Star Quilt Co. website. I went to the tutorials on YouTube and there was this lady named Jenny who kept showing all these fast and fun things to sew and quilt. I watched for a few days and said, "Why not me?! Heck, the worst that can happen is it isn't easy enough for me and I will have to find something else to fill my time."

So I bought a new machine, started watching the Daily Deals on the MSQC website, ordered some fabric, and started sewing. I am having a great time! I do use my seam ripper quite a bit and I have to wear a

magnifying headpiece to see what I am doing, but I'm sewing again.
I am amazed to be making quilts that I would never have even tried
when I had 20/20 vision. They're not perfect, but I look at all my little
mistakes as my signature. So thank you Jenny and your staff for all the
great tutorials and for convincing me that I can and do have the will and
capability to continue doing what I love.

The Best Snow Day

by **KARIN WOLFF**
Goshen, Kentucky

In preparation for my return to the United States after a long stint abroad, I asked my husband pretty please to place a fabric order to Missouri Star Quilt Company so that I could start sewing as soon as I got home! It was to be sent to our post office box. Unfortunately, I arrived back in Kentucky during a massive snowstorm that hit us in January. I was also unlucky enough to have a taxi driver who was not familiar with how far away our home was from the airport. A few minutes into the drive he asked me how much further it was, and I gave him the answer that I always gave the children when they asked, "Not much further now." But it was actually quite a ways away!

By the time I got home, the snow was so bad that the taxi was unable to drop me off at my door. I was forced to walk the entire block back to my car through five inches of snow, dragging two suitcases, but my determination kept me going. I had only one thing on my mind: picking up my fabric order! I jumped into my car only to find out that I had not only one, but four flat tires! I quickly made an emergency phone call to my husband for help. He assured me that it was okay to drive the car to the gas station to fill the tires. Thankfully, the post office was on the way! With my fabric finally in hand, I got to the car only to realize that there was no way that I could drive further towards the gas station, so I headed back home to hibernate.

Two days later I emerged from the blizzard to fix the tires and pick up more sewing supplies. My two days spent snowed in ended up being the best sewing days I have ever had! Thank you Missouri Star Quilt Company!

Mother's Time

by **DENISE GRESENS**
Shreveport, Louisiana

After being introduced to my first Missouri Star Quilt Co. jelly roll tutorial and completing the quilt in the fall of 2014, I was immediately hooked on quilting. For Christmas that year I sewed a baseball quilt for my husband, two jelly roll quilts for my sister and sister-in-law, and a special quilt for my elderly mother.

My father, who passed nearly twenty years before, had opened a clock shop in his retirement and spent much of his time studying and repairing antique clocks, watches, and pocket watches. His passion for clocks was always apparent, as we had many clocks in our home from my childhood on. In honor of my father's relationship with clocks, I decided to make a quilt for my mother with various circular stitches and an appliqué clock face in one of them. A sewing center appliquéd the numbers of the clock face onto a circle within the quilt, and then I took it home and appliquéd the hands onto the clock.

My mother opened her present at Christmas and was immediately enamored with her quilt. A year or so later, she became ill and was forced to move from the hospital to a rehabilitation facility, then back to hospital, and so on. When it was clear she wasn't improving, my sister and I decided to bring her back home, where she wanted to be, with her beloved cat Betsy and around-the-clock care. On January 5, 2016, my mother passed away with her quilt and her precious cat by her side.

A few weeks later, I brought the quilt home to wash and to store. When I began to fold it, I noticed the time appliquéd onto the clock was 7:12, the exact time my mother passed away. I'm not sure if it was God or if it was my mother, but someone seemed to be letting me know that she is safe in her Heavenly Father's hands. That moment—and the quilt—have brought me a great sense of peace.

Labor of Love

by **PAM ROBERTS-MCDONALD**
Lynden, Ontario

If I was ever in trouble or needed help, I only had to call one person and he would drop everything and run to me. My father was a man of few words and they rarely were "I love you", but his actions showed me how much he cared.

My dad had a major operation scheduled and now I had eighteen hours to show him what he meant to me. His surgery was set. He was in the hospital and he was cold. His head and toes were especially cold. So, I knew I had to do something.

I left the hospital with one thing on my mind. I had to make sure that before he went in for surgery, he would have a quilt to keep him warm when he woke up. It was more than a mission to keep him warm, it was for me too. I had to do this. I told myself if I did and then he would be okay.

The problem was I had no idea how to make a quilt. I had sewn clothing and baby things, but a quilt felt like it was out of my league. On the way home, I stopped at his house and raided his closet for old clothing items, anything I could cut up and sew together. I even took socks!

Old flannel shirts, out-of-fashion ties, cozy sweaters, fleece pants—they all became the pieces of my quilt. I also included scraps from clothing, baby gifts, and blankets I had made to make it long enough to wrap over his head and under his feet. I didn't have anything big enough for the backing, so I had to cut up the dog beds I had just finished (sorry puppies!) and piece it together. I lined it with my grandmother's ancient thick flannel sheet—the kind they don't make anymore, but they're so soft and warm. I started out frenzied, anxious, and afraid for what the next day would bring. As I sewed, I felt calmer. Each seam got me closer to my goal. I worked all night. My husband wanted to help, but this was something I needed to do by myself. It kept me from worrying. It kept me busy. It was an eighteen-hour labor of love.

My dad had ten years with his thrown-together quilt. From the day he brought it home, he never used anything else; it was his favorite. He cuddled my babies in it and watched hockey with them as they grew, tucked under it. They were wrapped in his love. After he died, everyone wanted it. My mum hung onto it for the first year and then gave it back to us. We all want to use Grandad's Blanket, or GB as my children say. Their memories of him are tied to it and they are forever trying to sneak it to their rooms.

GB always makes it's way back to me though, because the family knows when I have it tucked around my head and under my toes that I just need a moment to remember him.

Doing Fine

by **BECKY PILAND**
Berryton, Kansas

N o one in my family uses needles to create art, but as long as can remember I have used these sharp, shiny metal objects to create fiber arts. Everywhere I go, I bring my latest creation to work on. You never know when you might have a few minutes to squeeze in a little quilting.

My mother was ill for much of her adult life, which meant an occasional hospital visit and I often accompanied her on these visits. She apologized about my taking time off from work to stay with her, but when I showed her my quilting she said, "Oh, you'll be fine."

My mother eventually passed. I continued to quilt, always carrying a project with me.

Several years later, it was discovered that I had breast cancer after a routine exam. I had two surgeries and then met with my chemotherapy oncologist. Of course, I had my quilting with me.

When my doctor opened the door to the examination room and saw me working on my quilt, the first thing he said was, "Oh, you're quilting! You're going to be fine." As it turned out, I was fine as I continued to quilt even through those months of chemo and radiation.

I am more than three years cancer-free and I continue to quilt. I have donated my quilts for various charities, including fundraisers for families with seriously ill children.

Yes, I will be fine. Quilting gives me an opportunity to create yet still provides an avenue to help others. I truly believe that when a person focuses on others, they worry less about themselves and are healthier because of it.

Yes, I am fine!

Sewing Pieces, Finding Peace

by **PAMELA WENTZ**
Gastonia, North Carolina

I began my quilting career about two years ago. My first quilt felt like a disaster; let's call it a"wonky log cabin." With time and practice my skills improved and my stepmom, Jo Ann, asked me if I wouldn't mind putting together some squares that her mother had started before she passed away in 2004. When we got around to pulling out the bag of squares in the spring of 2015, we found 25 beautiful squares that had been individually quilted using a candle wicking technique. She told me there was no rush to finish the quilt, so I continued with other projects, but always kept those squares on my mental "to do" list.

A few months later, I was diagnosed with breast cancer. When I announced that I had decided to go with a very aggressive treatment, a double mastectomy, Jo Ann was one of my strongest supporters. Following the October surgery, I was not able to manage putting a quilt

through my sewing machine for a few weeks, but eventually I got my strength back and started quilting again.

Thanksgiving came and Jo Ann was not herself. She had lost a lot of weight and was very weak. The following Saturday she called to tell me that she had been diagnosed with pancreatic cancer. After the initial shock, and some time to process what this really meant, I knew that I had to finish her mother's quilt right away. Jo Ann was going to need all the love and support she could get to fight this awful disease.

Jo Ann's mother was an outstanding seamstress. She could look at a dress on a mannequin and go home and make it without using a pattern. Being a beginner, I wasn't sure if I knew how the quilt was meant to go together, and I spent hours studying the three squares that had been basted together. As I tried to work out in my mind how to finish this quilt, I began to feel a calming, peaceful influence come over me. It was as if Jo Ann's mother was there guiding me along. Solutions and ideas just came to me. These feelings continued each time I worked on the quilt, and eventually I also found my own peace with the realization that Jo Ann would be seeing her mother soon, and that all would be well.

When I gave Jo Ann the quilt, I shared my story with her. Jo Ann, Dad, and I all had a nice cry over it. Jo Ann took the quilt with her to doctor's appointments, chemotherapy treatments, and eventually to the hospital where she passed away in February.

I am so thankful that I began my quilting career and was able to help Jo Ann find peace, love, and comfort in a quilt from her mother. I will always treasure this quilt and my fond memories of her.

Out of the Sewing Machines of Babes

by **EVELYN KRUPICKA**
Naperville, Illinois

My name is Evelyn and I am twelve years old. Over the past year, quilting has come to mean a lot to me. It started in the summer of 2015 when my grandmother, Mary, offered to teach me how to quilt. Before then, I had barely picked up a needle, let alone made an entire quilt. Grandmary helped me pick out a charm pack from her stash and taught me how to lay the squares out to see how each square would look next to the others. Once I had it organized the way I liked, Grandmary brought me down to her sewing machine and showed me how to chain piece the squares.

Sitting at the sewing machine ignited something inside of me. It started my passion for sewing that had been waiting all those years for a chance to come alive. Within a few weeks my lap quilt was done. I was excited to have made my first quilt, as an eleven year old. My sister really liked my quilt so she asked me to make one for her too. I worked for the next four months, sometimes on my own and sometimes with Grandmary's

help, to make my sister a lap quilt. I was able to finish it up in time to give it to her as a Christmas gift.

Then I wanted to make another quilt, so Grandmary let me choose more fabric out of her supply and gave me a pattern she had picked up. I made this quilt at home on my mom's machine, working after school and on weekends. Since paying for longarm quilting was adding up, I took the challenge upon myself to quilt it. I had found a stencil I liked with loops and curls. Using an MSQC tutorial, I learned how to baste and machine quilt. I sat down at the sewing machine eager to get it done, but I found free motion quilting too difficult. The material bunched up and it was hard to turn for the loops. Machine quilting stressed me out.

I was ready to quit when my mom suggested hand quilting. She found me her old quilting hoop that had been gathering dust in the basement, and helped me get started. I found that hand quilting helped get rid of stress and let me relax. I learned and found ways to stitch more quickly. As I moved along, my stitches got better and better and I grew more and more confident in my work. I found out how to listen to audiobooks using an app from my library and I was able to do my two favorite things at one time, quilting and reading.

Quilting has really touched my heart. It has been a useful skill for me to have, and those who are close to me have benefited from it. It is something I know I will continue to do throughout middle school, high school, college, and the rest of my life.

Closet Quilter

by **RONNIE SPILLERS**
Pensacola, Florida

My quilting journey is a bit different from most. My mother and grandmothers weren't quilters, as far as I know. Grandma Head was neighbor across the street who happened to run a local boarding house. She watched me often and was a great influence in my upbringing. I loved her very much. She cooked three meals a day on a wood stove for her boarders and did all her wash out back in a big black wash pot. She also had quilting bees and a linen closet filled with quilts stacked very neatly to the ceiling.

The boarding house had two long hallways with rooms on both sides. These long halls were perfect for running and playing chase with the boarders' kids. Grandma Head warned me many times to "Stop that running!" Well, as it turned out, I did not heed the warning, and back in those days folks did not spare the rod. Grandma Head never would have spanked me, but she did have a punishment in mind. This particular day her patience was wearing thin and I had been warned plenty of times. Man, the running that day was grand. Then, all of a sudden, here she came around the corner saying, "That's it, Ronnie Jean!" Now for my punishment. She locked me in the linen closet—a large closet about

four by six feet. There was a drop down light bulb to furnish a dim, but sufficient light. Being the stubborn little girl that I was, there was no crying or begging to get out. I made up my mind that I would stay quietly until she let me out. In the meantime, I started pulling down and looking at all the quilts stored there. I was absolutely amazed at all the beautiful patterns and fabrics. I just kept pulling out those quilts and making up stories about them. I really don't know how long she had the lock on, but I didn't care.

I know it's was a weird way to develop a love for quilts, but that is how I came to love them. Grandma Head said many years later that she thought I had gone to sleep that day, but when she opened that door and saw all those quilts down off the shelves and me in the middle of the pile, she could not punish me any further. She also said that I began to ask her the names of the patterns. From that day on I have loved quilts: new quilts, old quilts, ragged quilts, quilts that have been loved, show quilts, scrap quilts, modern quilts, traditional quilts, and basically ALL QUILTS. I've never seen a quilt I didn't like. Thank you Grandma Head for the quilt education.

Unique Beauty

---✳---

by **NAOMI LITTOLFF**
Alsace, France

I've always struggled with social interaction and making friends, and anything that involves small talk is a nightmare for me! Basically, all the things that most people take for granted take a huge amount of effort and energy for me. When I was growing up, nobody really knew why I felt this way. Family members and doctors just assumed I was a bit aloof and antisocial, and no one really thought twice about it. Things got worse and worse, and I fell into a black hole of depression. I felt ashamed at myself for being so weak, but I also felt like I had nobody to lean on, as I couldn't naturally form social bonds with my peers.

When I was fifteen, my worried parents took me to see a new doctor, and I was diagnosed with Asperger's syndrome, a mild form of autism. I was put on medication, and I started to get help: I met people like me, and I was taught how to interact with people in a way that would make me feel comfortable whilst still appearing "normal." In other words, I was able to fly under the radar!

This is when quilting came into my life. I'd been hand sewing for years, ever since my grandmother taught me when I was six. But it wasn't until I started to climb out of my depression and embrace myself (and all my quirks) that I really started quilting. Suddenly, I could let myself express my fascination with different fabrics with all their different colors and textures, and not worry about appearing "weird," or "spastic," or "retarded." For the first time, I could freely show my enthusiasm through quilting.

I started to make quilts that were a celebration of myself and of the way I see the world. I am naturally more sensitive to sounds, smells, and colors and all my quilts reflect the unique beauty that only I can see.

It may sound dramatic to say that quilting saved my life, but I really feel like it's true. It became a way for me to express myself, and thus accept myself. It also had the added bonus of creating a fun conversation topic to talk to people about, and instead of being speechless and bored, I could let my passion shine through.

Little Jenny

by **JUDY TRUDELL**
Edmonton, Alberta

I am not sure when or how my story began, but it has evolved into a beautiful daily ritual with my four-year-old granddaughter, Chloe. I care for Chloe during the day while her parents are at their respective jobs. I enjoy quilting, and Chloe, being the creative spirit that she is, soon wanted her own fabric and scissors, just like Grandma. Before too long, I taught her how to use my sewing machine, with supervision, of course, and now she sews little strips and squares, pretending they are sashing or half-square triangles.

After watching the Improv Tote tutorial, Chloe was immediately hooked on MSQC videos. Recently, when Chloe lost the privilege of using the iPad, she cried, saying how she would miss watching the tutorials. As Chloe watches Jenny on a daily basis, she has started imitating her, and now I refer to Chloe as "Little Jenny."

She takes any and all fabric that she can get her hands on and creates tutorials in our living room. Chloe introduces herself as Jenny from the Missouri Star Quilt Company and proceeds to demonstrate her skills,

always naming the quilt she will be "working on." She says things like "Now let's go to the sewing machine and sew these squares together." She proceeds to the coffee table and runs a coaster over her fabric then goes off to another table to press from the pretty side of the fabric. Of course she throws in, "Isn't this just darling?" She talks about the sashing strips and borders like she has been quilting for years. When she's finished, she points to an imaginary quilt hanging behind her and closes each tutorial with "I hope you have enjoyed this tutorial from the Missouri Star Quilt Company." It's so precious to watch!

Today, during her play, she introduced my husband to Cornerstone quilt blocks, giving him her explanation of how they are used and how to incorporate them into the sashing of the Ohio Star quilt block. He seemed genuinely impressed.

Chloe recently asked me if I could get her a Jenny costume, apron, and a wig so she could be a star just like her. She notices every little detail, like when Jenny has a bandaid, wondering if her rotary cutter injured her finger. She's also been asking for a measuring bracelet just like the one Jenny wears.

Watching Chloe develop new skills and increase in self-confidence and a love for quilting at such a young age has truly touched my heart. It has allowed us so much more special time together, which I hope will lead her on to lifelong skills and a love of quilting.

I Don't Sew

✶

by **PATTY MONDSCHEIN**
Lansdale, Pennsylvania

When I was a young girl in school, I did not take home economics. Instead, I chose vocational art. So while I didn't learn to cook or sew, I could tell you about the masters and mediums in the art world.

Years later, I became interested in counted cross stitch, while my husband would stitch on his loose buttons and do his own minor sewing repairs. Thank goodness he learned those tedious tasks in the Air Force because I DON'T SEW!

As we began to build our family, I spent quality time in the kitchen, slowly becoming a half decent cook and an avid baker. In between, I cross stitched beautiful birth samplers for each of my children.

Some of the crafty moms in my neighborhood decided to form a "Stitch and B*tch" group, consisting of knitters, cross stitchers, and quilters. They taught me how to knit lovely children's sweaters, but I resisted the quilters, because, as I said, I DON'T SEW!

Week after week, as my friends would progress in their quilt making, I marveled at how beautiful the fabrics were and how the blocks all fit together so nicely. I began to wonder if I too could create such incredible works of art, but I was hesitant because I DON'T SEW!

Shortly thereafter, I became pregnant with my only daughter. I pondered whether I should cross stitch a birth sampler, as I had done for my boys, or knit a baby outfit to welcome her into the world.

At that point, my Stitch and B*tch group insisted that I make a quilt for my daughter-to-be. They forced me into registering for a beginner's quilting class at the local fabric shop. They dragged me out of my element and took me fabric shopping.

They no longer wanted to hear me say "I DON'T SEW!"

I wasn't too far into the classes when I discovered that I had been bitten by the quilt bug! I fell more in love with each stitch, completing my quilt within that year, just in time for my daughter's birth.

My daughter's heirloom was my first and most treasured quilt. And, unlike my sons, she doesn't have a cross stitched birth sampler.

Many years have passed since that time and now all my children have quilts of their own, made by me. My husband is a Civil War fanatic, so the quilts I've made for him consist of 1800's reproduction fabric from that time period. There are quilts throughout my home, adorning the walls, draped over chairs, as table runners, and covering the beds.

And my husband still sews on his own loose buttons, because he knows that I DON'T SEW, I QUILT!

The Ritual of the Tomatoes

by **TERRI THOMAS**
Green River, Wyoming

In Southeastern Idaho the growing season is very short. We grew the usual garden vegetables with success, but if you wanted to harvest tomatoes, you would need to begin early and prolong the season by any means possible. For as long as I can recall, my father would perform what we liked to call "the ritual of the tomatoes."

In the spring, a little paper cap was put over each plant to protect it from freezing. Then, as the plant would mature, and after the danger of frost had passed, a wire cage would help support the fruit on each plant.

As summer turned into fall, it was time again to keep an eye on the temperature. If it was going to be 32 degrees or below, it was time to cover the tomatoes to protect them from freezing. There would still be many greenish-orange tomatoes on the vine just waiting for a few more warm days to ripen, our mouths watering in anticipation.

My father painted houses as a second job, so we were the lucky owners of large canvas tarps. The tarps were also used to protect our annual crop of tomatoes. Tarps were spread out over the garden, covering each tomato cage, turning our garden into a field of paint-spotted, gray, snow-covered bushes.

My in-laws also practiced the ritual of the tomatoes, nurturing them in the spring and then protecting them in the fall. I enjoyed very much going out to their garden. However, one fall brought a startling revelation.

Draped over tomato cages, tucked under tomato plants, and lying in mud at my in-laws' was not the usual paint-splattered tarp, but squares and triangles. I just stood there trying to comprehend what paint tarp would have squares and triangles all over it. Then I realized those squares and triangles were a pattern. What I saw spread out before me wasn't a paint tarp, but a hand-pieced quilt! I didn't know what to do! I ran into the house to ask someone where the quilts had come from. It turns out they had been hand-pieced in Iowa by my mother-in-law's grandmother and they had been made just for her!

Thankfully, those quilts are no longer protecting tomatoes, but are being protected themselves. What pieces we could salvage were then made into works of art to enhance the walls of their home.

That was many years ago, but today my mother-in-law speaks fondly of those quilt blocks hanging on her wall and feels a strong connection with her grandmother. Never again will the ritual of the tomatoes be graced with a hand-pieced quilt. At least not in our family!

A Sewing Machine in Iraq

by **DEBBY WHEELOCK**
Bedford, Indiana

I've been sewing for over twenty six years. After I got married, I was given a old sewing machine by my mother-in-law. The machine, my beloved Singer, was made the same year I was born. I have sewn many quilts in my day and I just love working with fabrics. No one in my family sews, I just took to it and taught myself how to do things.

In 2008, I deployed to Iraq and one thing I insisted on was no boring tour for me. Before going to Iraq, I was stationed in Fort Stewart, Georgia, for two and a half months of combat training. We earned a four day pass and my family came down to visit. I went to a local Walmart and bought a sewing machine. My husband took it home and I gave him my new address for Iraq, so when I got there, my sewing machine was waiting on me. I made all kinds of fabric bags for soldiers to take to the embroiderer and have designs put on them for their wives, which made me feel good. The fabric was sent from home and it was the Army digital camouflage pattern.

I was then put to work sewing and repairing uniforms, so the quilt tops I wanted to make had to be put on hold. I stayed pretty busy and no one could believe I had a sewing machine in my room. When August rolled around, I started packing up things early to send home since we were leaving Iraq in late November. There's a rule that when you send items home you can't tape up the box because a postal employee must check every item to make sure you are not sending home something not allowed. I told him what was in the box, but he did not believe me until he saw it for himself. He said, "I have seen many things come through here, but this is a first for me." Most likely the last too.

I often wonder what my time in Iraq would have been like without that sewing machine. But let's not think about that since I would not have been able to share my story with you!

A Distraction

by **LYNN BAKER**
Phoenixville, Pennsylvania

Three years ago, my husband and I decided to start having the children we had always talked about. After a year without results, we sought help. I was diagnosed with polycystic ovary syndrome. The only way I would be able to have children was with medical intervention. A year and a half after starting to try, we began fertility treatments.

This was a rough time for us. I was an emotional mess from all the hormones and I was struggling with my identity as a woman and a wife. All of the negative pregnancy tests month after month were devastating. My husband was amazingly supportive and loving, as were my wonderful friends who prayed and cried with me and were there for me through everything.

In March of 2015, we decided that if this latest round of treatments didn't work we were done. Easter morning I woke up feeling weird and wanted to take yet another pregnancy test, only I was scared to see another negative result. I didn't want to be an emotional mess for church or family, so I didn't take the test.

The next day I had a day off from work. I felt weird again and decided to take a pregnancy test. To my utter disbelief it was positive! After so many negative tests I couldn't believe it. I figured it was a faulty test, but I didn't have another to verify and my doctor didn't have an opening until the next day. I had an entire day home, alone, and I was in desperate need of something to take my mind off of the following day's appointment.

So, I got out my 1950's cast iron Singer and a poor excuse for a jelly roll. I turned on YouTube to Missouri Star Quilt Company's channel and watched Jenny sew a jelly roll race quilt. I watched the video so many times that day, rewinding and rewatching the same parts, as I put together my very first quilt to keep my mind off of whether or not I was pregnant.

That first day I completed the main part of the quilt. The following day was my appointment. I was sent on my way with the promise of a phone call later with the results. The results came back positive; I was pregnant! Over the next couple of months, as I had to fight not to call my mom with the news too early, I spent my time bordering, machine quilting, and binding. I learned through that time that I love quilting.

A year after starting my first quilt, I have one quilt finished, I own a new sewing machine, I'm halfway through my second quilt, I'm starting a quilting group at my church, and I have a beautiful, healthy baby girl. What a difference a year makes! Quilting started as a distraction from my personal struggles and has turned into a beloved hobby.

Back to Life

by **MARY BETH WEEKS**
Homer Glen, Illinois

Several years ago, I was ill for an extended period of time. My life consisted pretty much of shuffling between the bed and the sofa. I had long hours of free time, but no hope of being able to do what I most loved: making quilts. But those unfinished projects piled in my upstairs sewing room were never far from my mind and I yearned to bring them to life again. Then inspiration struck; why not sew in the dining room?! I wasn't going to be serving dinners in there anytime soon. My daughter and husband were most cooperative. They hauled down my sewing machine, cutting tools, ironing board, endless gadgets, as well as piles and bins of fabric and, of course, the unfinished projects.

I could tolerate working about 15 minutes at a time. I learned to iron sitting down. As I worked on my various quilts in this way for more than a year, I found it to be liberating and life affirming. I had accomplished something by the end of each day. I once again felt the satisfaction and joy of a finished quilt project. My daughter was thrilled with the Bargello wall quilt I completed for her office. When my guild did a mystery quilt, I was able to participate. I made charity quilts. I had something cheerful to mention when talking to friends and family and they got excited for me as well.

This was not only therapy for me, it was therapy shared. I was sewing again and surely all was right with the world. Eventually I grew stronger and moved back into my upstairs sewing room. However, I no longer accumulate partially finished projects on my shelves. Everything started is a work in progress until it's finished and somehow that feels therapeutic too!

Bingo!

by **YVONNE ROMANN**
Perryville, Missouri

"Bingo?!" I yelled with a question in my voice. Had I really won a quilt? It was the Annual Seminary Picnic in Perryville, Missouri, in the late 1970's. Playing bingo for one of those beautiful quilts was a favorite way to donate to the local church. Back then, and still today, the ladies of the church gathered weekly to help complete the handmade quilts needed for the picnic bingo. "Bingo!" I kept hearing my voice echo in my head. Me? I don't like to play bingo, but to donate to the church I had bought $20 worth of tickets to play that silly game. My head still spinning from hearing the word "bingo," I was rather embarrassed when this beautiful quilt was placed in my arms. So I sat there playing the rest of the games I had purchased with the $20. I was bored, but began to feel like I had done something wrong by winning that lovely quilt. So I bought another $20 worth of quilt tickets and then sat playing those cards. With just $40 I had won my first and only quilt while playing bingo. This beautiful embroidered quilt had a special place in my closet. It was kept in a safe place to secretly admire since it was my only time ever to win at bingo.

Snow and ice jeopardized our daughter's travel plans in the winter of 1980. She was attending college in St. Louis, almost a two-hour drive from our home in Perryville, Missouri. Since the weather threatened to halt traffic, we encouraged her to prepare to leave for school early. As she carried belongings to her car, I suggested she take an old quilt along, just in case of trouble along the way. After a short argument that she would not need a quilt, she finally headed for the quilt closet. After another short argument about which quilt to take with her, she carried my never-used "bingo" quilt to her car. There were no cell phones back then to keep in touch, so she promised to call me soon as she arrived at school.

With a sigh of relief, I answered her telephone call a couple of hours later. She was sobbing uncontrollably, "Mom, I am so sorry. I promise I will listen to you the next time." She continued, "I was one of the first to arrive at a terrible wreck where this man was lying in the ice and snow. He was going into shock and I used your quilt to keep him warm. When the ambulance arrived, they kept him wrapped in the quilt and it is gone."

Everything has a purpose in this world. That quilt had served its purpose. "Bingo!"

Quilting with Pappy

by **CATHEY RANDOLPH**
San Antonio, Texas

I was a newlywed in 1975 and I wanted to make a quilt for my new bed. My grandmother and grandpa, Pappy, came from Shawnee, Oklahoma, to San Antonio, Texas, to help me make a quilt. I spent quite a bit of time with them growing up and in college, so this visit was very special.

We had just purchased a king-sized bed, but I didn't have a single king quilt for it and that bothered me! I had slept under one of Granny's quilts practically every night of my life.

I hand cut all the blocks and strips while Granny pieced it on the sewing machine, teaching me at every step. When it was time to quilt it, she pulled out her quilting frame and we got after quilting it by hand.

My Pappy was very interested in the process, even though he had seen it a thousand times before. He had Alzheimer's by then and tended to wander off, but every day was a new day of discoveries. Granny loved to quilt and he kept bothering her, but she didn't want him to wander off while we were quilting, so she gave him a threaded needle and put him to work. She told me Pappy had never participated before, but was always quick to comment on her technique in the past. He sat down and got after it!

Granny saw Pappy's work, and told me later that she would remove his long stitches and replace them with her tiny even stitches. I told her to leave them alone because no quilt is ever perfect and Pappy was having fun. She laughed and then sighed and said that if he made any stitches longer than 3⁄8 of an inch, she wouldn't be able to control herself or the seam ripper.

My Granny, Pappy, Mom, and I quilted for days. Pappy really stuck with it and stayed on the drawn-in quilting pattern lines pretty good. His stitches varied in length quite a bit, but he was proud of them. He only got up to go outside and stretch his legs or to get a snack—or yell at my grandfather clock. When it would strike, he would go over and look at that clock and tell it, "You are the ugliest woman I have ever seen, and you're too damn loud." Pappy never cussed, so this was particularly amusing. Then he would come over and sit back down and quilt like nothing ever happened.

Needless to say, Granny and Pappy went to Heaven long ago. I still have the "Pappy clock" and that beautiful quilt with all the quilting perfection of my Granny and haphazard stitching of my Pappy. At night I sleep peacefully with the memories of making the quilt I am sleeping under, as well as Pappy cussing out the grandfather clock chiming in the front room. When I make my bed I notice the imperfect stitches and remember how truly blessed I am.

The Blue and Yellow Quilt

by **ANNA MUSCATO**
Tonawanda, New York

My mother could sew, but she never really put her talent to use until my first baby was about to be born. She hid the fact that she had a precious quilt in the works for my firstborn, her first grandchild. I was amazed when she gave this sweet little blue and yellow crib quilt to me and placed it center stage in the nursery, awaiting the time when my son Christopher would be born.

That quilt went everywhere: to the grocery store, to the dentist, and it was always under his head at night to soften his sleep. Years passed by quickly and that quilt continued to get plenty of use—and I kept on washing his quilt. When Christopher was in high school, he would still sleep with the quilt under his head before a big game to give him luck.

Then, when he went off to college, the first thing he packed was his little blue and yellow quilt. I asked him, "Are you really going to take that quilt to college? You are staying in a dorm room." His simple answer was,

"Yes, it's mine." Looking into his eyes, I again saw him as a little child saying, "Mine, Mommy!"

Our first visit to his college was exciting and we took the whole family. There in his dorm room hanging up to dry was his tattered little blue and yellow quilt that his grandmother, Nanny Be, made twenty years ago just for him. It was hanging up there in front of the dorm crowd of big college boys and no one said a word about it. After all, it belonged to a big tough football player. Who would ever argue with him? He would look at them as if to say, "It's mine. Nanny Be made it and don't say another word about it."

I managed to get him to part with it for a little while just so I could take it home to sew a few new patches on it and new binding. The only reason he parted with it was I promised him that it would last longer if he let me fix it.

Our next destination directly after visiting Christopher was Disney World. He had exams so he couldn't come. The rest of us, my husband, my daughter Samantha, and my other son Justin, took the little blue and yellow quilt went on our way. When it was time for bed, there weren't enough pillows in the hotel, so Samantha used Christopher's quilt for a pillow. Unfortunately, that quilt was left behind when we were packing for home! My first thoughts were along the lines of, "We are all dead when Chris finds out!" That next morning the first thing I did was call Disney World. I explained my dilemma to the sweet lady in housekeeping, leaving out the fact my son was nineteen years old. Her question was, "Will the baby be able to sleep without his blankie tonight?" I said that he wouldn't and she sent the quilt overnight to us.

We all survived the college years. Then Christopher brought another addition to our family, his wife Heather. Years went by and I quite frankly forgot about his quilt. Then one day I overheard Heather's sister saying, "What's with that little baby blanket?" Heather said, "Don't let Chris hear you call it a blanket! It's a quilt made by his Nanny. Help me pack for our move, but don't touch the quilt." I'd even heard that the prenuptial agreement for Chris and Heather's marriage included the little blue and yellow quilt—that it would come along always with no questions asked.

Thirty eight years after Christopher was born, a new addition came to our family: his little daughter Sophia. Sophia is so precious to us; she was born with Cystic Fibrosis and we all work hard to keep her healthy. Now she calls me Nanny and I've made her a one-of-a-kind quilt. She is doing well. I also make quilts to raise donations to find the cure for my special girl Sophia. And, believe it or not, on Christopher and Heather's bed is that little blue and yellow quilt made for him forty three years ago by his Nanny Be.

Finding Sanity

by **KELLY LACINA**
St. Joseph, Missouri

L ife got interesting really quick. After having four babies in five and a half years, the fourth, Kristine, was born with Down syndrome, autism, and selective mutism. Then, a year and a half later, the oldest, Katherine, was surprisingly diagnosed with Unverricht-Lundborg syndrome, a very rare form of neurodegenerative epilepsy. Neurodegeneration means her brain is slowly dying.

My hands were full and I was overwhelmed. I needed help getting through the challenges I was facing. Then my best friend, Jacque, showed up with a needle, thread, and fabric and said I was going to piece a pillow top. I thought to myself that the last thing I needed was something else to do! My time was already full of cloth diapers, trips to the library, healthy snacks, kid crafts, plus the addition of hours upon hours of hospital and doctor visits, and speech and physical therapy appointments every week. Jacque was proposing a time-consuming addition to my schedule. As only a close friend could though, she recognized the onset of a little mommy insanity! Unknowingly, she was

also inviting me to return to my roots. My grandmother had lovingly taught me to embroider when I was eight. Grandma thought it would be an activity that would hold us together, because my parents were moving our family from near her home in California, clear out to snow-covered Missouri!

I accepted Jacque's pillow top pieces and found myself loving the few minutes each week when I had a needle in my hand. Then I started to think that maybe Jacque was right, I needed some time to create, time just for me. The next thing she had the audacity to propose was attending a quilt guild one entire evening a month! Again, who has the time? Jacque was persistent. I attended a meeting. I also began stitching while waiting during medical appointments and I found it soothing to my soul. Jacque's next lifesaving idea—and she was saving my life, I just did not recognize how deep I was in—was to say, "It's only overnight and a few miles from home, let's go on a quilt retreat!" I couldn't leave my loving husband with four young children. He said, "Go!" Perhaps, he recognized the insanity, too.

Medical bills were piling up. Jacque said the retreat was a gift and also gave me her old sewing machine, because mine was, well, decrepit! While attending I finished a small project. This retreat caught me falling in love with petting material and with another quilter's kaleidoscope flannel quilt. Mounting, humongous medical bills and a craving for flannel are not are not compatible! But when I walked into the next quilt guild meeting, I found pieces of flannel stacked up on the table and chair next to Jacque. The other retreat quilters were now feeding my addiction and making it possible for me to complete my first quilt, besides teaching me that the sisterhood of quilters is life-giving!

Grandma's needle and thread followed me across the country through motherhood, into the sometimes-heartbreaking, yet rewarding, world of children with special needs, and right into the arms of loving friends and sanity!

The Joy of Quilting

by **GLEN DAVIS**
Pratt, Kansas

My story starts in 1993 when my wife, Jan, and I took a quilting class offered in the evening at the school where we taught. We each made a small wall hanging. It was back when the country style of decorating was popular and our wall hangings were cows! We continued to dabble in quilting for the next few years, but Jan was mostly into sewing stuffed animals and crafts. In 2004, we were working on a quilt together when Jan was diagnosed with cancer. We spent a month at MD Anderson Cancer Center in Houston and, of course, took our sewing machine, rotary cutter, and fabric and worked on a quilt in the hotel room between her doctor's appointments. We finished the top before we headed home to meet with an oncologist. He told us that it was too late to do any treatments and Jan died at home two weeks later.

After Jan's death, I continued to work on quilts for our three boys and for friends that had been so supportive throughout the years. In 2005, the boys and I moved to Pratt, Kansas, Jan's hometown, to be near their grandmother, and I took a position as superintendent of the Pratt

schools. One day I got an email from Joy Kahmeyer, one of the English teachers, noting that she had heard I was a quilter and asked if I would like to trade some "stash." I did and I also joined a small quilting group of teachers who met on Wednesday evenings. In September I got an email from Miss Kahmeyer asking if I would like to go with her to the State Fair to look at the quilt entries. I said yes! In 2007 Joy Kahmeyer and I were married. It was her first marriage at age sixty!

In our nine years of marriage, we have really gotten into quilting. We have four rooms filled with our fabric stash. I have a longarm quilting business and a featherweight collection, and we have an online "I spy" quilt kit business. We love to quilt and most quilts we make we give to friends or charities for fund raisers. Tonight we are finishing a t-shirt quilt for the "Builders for Christ" church teams that came to Pratt, Kansas, last summer and built our new sanctuary at First Southern Baptist Church.

I would definitely say that quilting has brought "joy" to my life and helps me cherish memories of my past.

Quilting Mischief

by **REGINA THURBER**
South Portland, Maine

A few years ago, I decided to make my husband a flannel lap quilt for his birthday. February in Maine tends to be a bit nippy and I knew he'd love something to snuggle up in.

I thought I had enough flannel to work with, but when I checked my stash, I realized I did not. Since I was using plaid flannel I figured I could use some of his flannel shirts to bridge the gap. I was pretty sure he would never miss them, or even know that the quilt had quite a bit of his shirts in it.

His closet was jam-packed with flannel shirts and, feeling devilish, I thought I would hang some of the shirts back in his closet with giant square holes in them. I knew he planned on cleaning out his closet come spring, so I eagerly anticipated the moment when he would discover the shirts.

When he finally found the shirts, he hollered out to me asking if we had moths that chewed square holes in his shirts. I was laughing so hard, all I could do was hold up his quilt pointing to the squares that matched his shirt! Thankfully he laughed along with me. It has been a favorite story around here for some time now!

Full

by **LUCILLE WARD**
Santa Cruz, California

I live in Santa Cruz, California, and it is a city filled with wonderful bakeries. My favorite is called "The Buttery." I am a regular patron and I stop in at about 8:30 a.m. each morning for a cup of coffee and a treat.

One such morning, I was sitting at the community table and seated next to me was a couple, slightly older than me, having a breakfast of cherry pie with whipped cream and a latte. "Impressive breakfast," I commented. A conversation ensued, we introduced ourselves, and her husband returned to his crossword puzzle. That's when I met my friend Sandy.

Sandy and I were both in our seventies. I was newly retired and she asked if I had a bucket list. I replied that I didn't. I did, however, have a closet full of fabric. I explained that I'd stopped sewing when I started working full time and now that I had the time, I would like to learn to quilt. Her face lit up as she explained that she was a quilter and invited me over to her house to learn with her.

For the next two years we met at least once a week. During that time I made numerous table runners, three baby quilts, and five full-sized quilts. Sandy shared her quilting supplies, her time, and her expertise. She heaped praise on my projects, even though the first few projects were not really praiseworthy. We sewed and shared stories about our lives and our values. She was kind, encouraging, and validating.

Early in 2015, Sandy was diagnosed with cancer. We continued to quilt once a week. When the treatments proved fruitless, she taught me about grace under fire, about holding on and letting go. Amazingly, she planned her last project, a king-sized quilt with a very challenging pattern, and asked me, if necessary, to finish the quilt for her. Of course I said yes, and then prayed night and day that she would be able to finish the quilt. Well, Sandy finished that quilt and even made a second "last" quilt. I did finish her very last project, a table runner she was making for me.

Sandy did not die with a closet full of quilts. Every quilt was made with a recipient in mind. She never sold her quilts; like her quilting talent, they were gifts to be shared.

On July 30th, Sandy's birthday, I'll be at The Buttery. I'll have cherry pie with whipped cream and a latte, celebrating the wonderful friend who made me a quilter.

No Whining

by **CARLA SOARES AND DEBRA BOPP**
Imperial, Nebraska

My mother was diagnosed with cancer for the second time in December of 2005. We had been through this before and knew this time would be the last. My sister, Carla, decided to fly back to Nebraska to spend time with Mom and me. To keep our minds occupied we decided to make a quilt to pass the time. My sister had purchased a block of the month the year before and brought it for us to work on. Our mom was able to watch us work on the blocks. We told her we would use it as a raffle quilt for my sister's local Relay for Life in California where she lived.

Our mother passed away in December 2006, never having seen the completed quilt, but knowing what it would be used for. She always told us to put on our big girl panties and not to whine about her prognosis. We named the finished quilt "No Whining" as the theme of the quilt was grapes and wine bottles, stitched in purples and greens, which Mom loved. Tickets were sold and we made close to $1,700 for the Relay for Life. I flew to California to participate in the drawing. It went to a lady

my sister knew who lived in a city about 90 miles from her. She was thrilled and loved the quilt!

Fast forward four years to 2011. My sister went to work and there was a box waiting for her with her name on it. When she opened it, there was Mom's quilt with a letter from the owner. She wrote that in 2009, her home had caught on fire. It started in the living room where the quilt was draped over her couch. When the firefighters arrived, the first place they aimed their hoses was at the couch. Her entire living room was destroyed except a few mementos and that quilt. The quilt itself is still in perfect condition, not even the slightest hint of smoke. Talk about a miracle. She said every time she wrapped herself in the quilt she could feel our love and thought it should be returned back to us.

My sister kept this a secret until she came back to Nebraska to go to Quilt Nebraska with me. There, at the evening of show and tell, she got up and told this story and how the quilt came back home to us. She renamed the quilt "Coming Home" and presented it to me, saying that I deserved to have it as I was Mom's caregiver and the glue that held us together when our world fell apart. It had gone through fire to come home to us. Needless to say there wasn't a dry eye in the room after her presentation. It was a wonderful moment. We both still quilt and share ideas, but this quilt will always be special to us.

As Good As It Gets

by **URSULA BEYELER**
Aarwangen, Belgium

In 1982, after finishing commercial trainee time and earning some money, us two Swiss girls planned a trip abroad. While checking out locations and schools—It was quite a task, there was no Internet yet—we discovered that Ireland had all the amenities one could wish for. In March we both quit our jobs. Only days before we left I met my future husband. Madly in love, I could barely stand the thought of being away from him. Still, we went ahead with our plans and left Switzerland in April.

The journey was an adventure in itself. Flying was out of the question. So we traveled by train through Switzerland, Germany, and France, then took the ferry from Calais to Dover, and continued by train to Pembroke in Wales and boarded yet another ferry to Cork in the south of Ireland. We arrived in Cork Harbor utterly exhausted. Only the excitement of the new surroundings kept us awake. A taxicab brought us to our respective addresses. When I rang the doorbell of my future home, I was greeted by a woman with a warm smile and in this very moment, I knew that I had struck gold! Ina and I bonded instantly.

In the following 9 months we attended school, discovered the breathtaking beauty of the Emerald Isle, and got ready for our English papers. While my friend was mixing with art and music students and went as far as leasing an apartment with a group of girls she met at University, I became a full member of my Irish family—Ina, Paddy, her husband, three adorable children, their grandparents, and uncles and aunts. Ina had worked as a dressmaker before becoming a stay-at-home mum and did odd jobs for friends and neighbors. I particularly remember a lovely floral dress she created for a four-year-old girl. It was made of beautiful cotton fabric with matching ribbons and lace. This was the first time I'd ever heard the name "Laura Ashley."

Later she showed me the tiny cramped fabric shop in Cork. I had no idea that patterns and colors could be combined in such ways. There were packets of hexagons and Ina demonstrated that one was to sew them

together by hand and she drew out the pattern of how it was supposed to look when finished. Of course all you American Quilters know a Grandmother's Flower Garden quilt, but for this 20-year-old Swiss girl, a whole new world had just opened up.

December came and with it the English exams in Dublin and a tearful goodbye. In the decades to come there was a lot of traveling back and forth, not to mention letter exchanges. Despite the booming Internet, we still used up a lot of ink. Losses were mourned together and weddings were attended here and there. When I became a stay at home mum myself, I started to sew for our girls. And I gave my first quilt a try: a Log Cabin style quilt in Laura Ashley fabric. It was done with a lot of pinning and ripping. I even made cardboard templates and dealt with metric measurements!

From then on I laid my hands on everything I could get about quilts: books, patterns, magazine articles, and so on. I grew more confident. The pins became less and with the ¼" foot I abandoned the metric system. Boy, what a relief! I found Jenny on YouTube and became familiar with yet another language, "Quiltish." Because of Jenny, I applied for my very first credit card. I'll never forget the thrill when our postman brought the first parcel with the MSQC star on it.

Meanwhile, Ina is a grandmother now with four grandchildren. It's needless to say what the birthday gifts were. My dearest friends all have quilts by now and every new baby in our neighborhood gets one. I like to make classic patterns as well as improvisational projects and I read a lot about quilting.

Two of my friends got the quilting bug because of the YouTube videos I kept showering them with and we formed a quilting bee together. Lately I've discovered 1930's reproduction fabrics and that Grandmother's Flower Garden quilt is still on my mind.

I'd like to thank Jenny and the Doan Family, and all the busy people at MSQC, for the happiness and the challenging projects that they've brought to me.

A Sweet Memory

by **DANIELLE STIMPSON**

A Last fall I helped my good friend make her very first quilt for her soon-to-be-born son. We shopped together to find the perfect prints and colors. I taught her about half-square triangles and we planned out the perfect pattern. We embroidered his name and due date on the top of his quilt. Then we ended up picking out the previous date and embroidering a new date as he had decided to come to Earth early. He was a perfect baby, always happy, always joyful. She loved wrapping him in his special quilt.

Sadly, he had to leave the Earth nearly as quickly as he came. As his mother grieved, some good friends and I stayed up late each night, working around the clock, and used the scraps of her first quilt to make this sweet baby a quilt to be buried in. At his funeral she clung to the quilt she had so lovingly made for him. Today, his quilt is kept in her living room for her family to see and snuggle anytime they need to, so they can remember this sweet baby and the love they all shared together.

Shining Happy Quilting

---

by **BONNIE HOOLEY (SCRAPPY SISTERS)**
Winnipeg, Manitoba

Many people would think I am exaggerating this story, but my friends and my teacher, who knows me well, can vouch for me when it comes to my sewing adventures.

I saw a picture of a quilt on Facebook and thought, "I should try that." I am a scrap quilter and the design was perfect! I figured out the pattern and started going through my stash for the perfect fabrics.

Now, if you knew me you would know that much of my stash comes from Faye bags. Faye bags are scraps bags I buy at my favorite quilt shop: "Faye's Henhouse." They are small brown paper bags filled with numerous pieces of fabric of different colors, shapes, and sizes. I dug through my stash looking for colorful pieces and white scraps of fabric for contrast.

Some of the white pieces that I found had a slight sheen on one side. They were definitely cotton and not too glitzy to stand out, so I included them to add interest. And add interest they did!

After much sewing and cutting, it was time to press the seams. There were a lot to press because I had learned the art of chain stitching. Much more gets done before pressing happens when you chain stitch.

I was chatting with my sister Kathy, a fellow quilter, on the phone when I began to iron. To my horror, the nicely sewn block had melted to my iron and left behind the ghastly smell of glue! I told Kathy what was happening and she laughed until she cried, while I protested it was not funny.

It turns out those nice shiny pieces in my stash were not fabric, but iron on interfacing!

Refusing to admit defeat, I took a piece of cloth and ironed off the glue from each tainted block—after all white fabric is still fabric.

My finished project is extra special now because when I look at it, I know the story and the "real" work that went into making it!

Kindred Cattails

by **CHRISTA MARCOTTE**
Torquay, Saskatchewan

For the past six years, my quilting friends and have made the trek down from Saskatchewan to Montana once a year for the Makoshika quilt show in Glendive. You don't have to twist our arms as The Enchanted Room is 7,000 bolts of fabulousness and Laura is such a great shopkeeper.

One year, we offered to send down some quilts for a Canadian exhibit in their show. That's when I met Pat for the first time. She and I had made the same quilt by Judy Niemeyer called "Cattails." She had made hers into irises and I had stuck with the original design. She won second and I won third. We challenged each other to make a Mariner's Compass quilt for the following year. It was a friendly competition as we didn't know each other very well, but looked forward to meeting up the next spring.

I had a chance to stop at The Enchanted Room on a trip that fall and I asked Laura how Pat was doing with her quilt. She had told me that

just two weeks prior, Pat had come to the store with her husband and purchased a new Judy Niemeyer kit called "Glacier Star" and was saying how this quilt was going to be for herself. But as Pat got in the truck to go home, she suffered a massive stroke and was rushed to the hospital. She had a long road to recovery ahead of her. Laura and I cried together. I hardly knew Pat, but it still brought tears to my eyes. I was so sad for this kindred farm wife that I had felt such a connection to. When we regained composure, I heard myself say, "Tell Pat that I will make her quilt for her." Laura's jaw dropped. I said, "Really. I mean it." I don't know many people who actually complete a Judy Niemeyer quilt and I wanted Pat to have it so that she could snuggle under a quilt she loves during her recovery.

I wondered if I would ever see this kit that I'd promised to make. I could imagine their thoughts. Send it to Canada? To a total stranger? Are we ever going to see it again? But shortly after, the kit showed up in the mail. I pieced it, paid to have it custom quilted, and sent it back to Pat. We met up again last spring and spent some time together as we enjoyed the quilt show. Pat would not use her quilt until it was hung at this show! I was so glad to be able to help Pat with her recovery in the best way I know how, with quilting!

Quilting is for Boys Too!

by **AIDAN EDMONDS**

I love quilting. I believe quilting is not for just girls and old ladies. It encompasses everyone, even ten-year-old boys.

The first quilt I ever made was a very small quilt for my new baby sister. My grandmother helped me make it. It was a pink and blue nine patch. It had a textured brown backing. I also free quilted a flower on it. My baby sister loved it!

I decided for my next quilt that I wanted more of a challenge. I made a twelve square animal quilt. I made twelve different textured animal squares with my grandma. I enjoyed spending the time with her. My mom taught me how to piece it together. It was a fun and educational experience.

I think quilting is an amazing form of art. I like quilting because you can take a meaningless piece of fabric and make it into a meaningful piece of art.

Aidan, age 10

Sewn Together

by **SUSAN GRAVEDONI**
Petoskey, Michigan

I must to share the story of how quilting touched my life. In December 2014, I was diagnosed with an early stage of breast cancer. It was scary for me; I was only fifty one years old.

I followed my treatment plan and by February 2015, I was done. How lucky was I to have this behind me?! In May 2015, I quit my job to take time for myself and my family, and to spend more time with my aging parents. My mom had suffered a stroke two years prior and she recovered quite remarkably, but she still struggled with some things, like her quilting.

In September, I joined my mom's quilting group. It was a group of about twenty people that made quilts for the beds at our local hospice house. Each family got to take home a quilt. I did not sew, but I joined as the "gopher." I would sort the fabric, iron, cut, take pictures, iron on labels, and help with any chore that was needed to be done so that the ladies could sew, sew, sew.

Well, that didn't last long. After my first day, I was sent home with a simple pattern, some Christmas fabrics, and all the supplies to make it. I wanted to try it. I wanted to create my own masterpiece and be like these talented, creative, amazing, quilting ladies. I borrowed a machine. I watched many tutorials. I had to learn everything! I laughed at the names of fabric precuts: jelly rolls, layer cakes, turnovers, they all sounded yummy to me.

My Christmas quilt was finished mid-December. Woohoo! It wasn't perfect, but the ladies informed me that's why it's called a quilt! I did it! I was hooked. I was giving back to the community and I was also spending quality time with my mom.

Then boom! In late December, a new cancer had appeared in me. How? Why? It couldn't be possible. I was facing a bilateral mastectomy in February, 2016. On a happier note, we also found out we were going to be grandparents in June! I became obsessed with my quilting projects. I found it to be the best therapy; I could easily get lost in my projects.

The fabric selection let my mind create beautiful visions and stop thinking about the ugly cancer in my body. Cutting let me focus on strips, squares, and inches and not the size of my tumor. Sewing kept me focused, staying on task, not the thoughts of cancer running through my body. Ripping out seams helped me to release my anger. Pressing the perfect seam was soothing and comforting. The end result was a beautiful quilt for a family that had just lost a loved one. I did not let worries about the future enter my little quilting room.

It has been two weeks since my surgery. I have completed three quilts. I never would have dreamed that I would have cancer, that my parents would get older, that I would be a grandma, or that I would be quilting. All these life changing events, and my quilting debut, have been perfectly sewn together.

Aloha

by **MARYANN ROYLO**
Cranberry Township, Pennsylvania

I n early 2008, I retired due to medical issues after being a nurse in Hawaii for forty two years. I was left with an empty feeling as I wondered what I could do now with my rather sedentary life. One day I read in the newspaper about a family, previously homeless, who had finally gotten a home through Habitat for Humanity. I knew this family! They had lived on a North Shore beach not far from the community hospital where I worked. I had taken care of the children when they came to the ER. Many years later, I also took care of the now grown sisters when they delivered their babies at the same hospital.

According to the article, there were ten children between the two sisters, who now had a home with seven bedrooms located on the west side of the island. A light bulb went off in my head. I would make a quilt for each one of the children! Luckily, there was a picture of the family included in the article and between that and the information that I had received from Habitat for Humanity, I had the names and ages of the children. I started in spring with the hope of completing the quilts by Christmas. The plan was to drop them off at Habitat for Humanity.

At that time quilting was fairly new to me, so I decided to make simple quilts, mostly whole cloth quilts, using novelty prints or patterns that were easy to machine quilt. I surprised myself when I finished them all by September. I notified Habitat for Humanity in December that I was dropping off the quilts and hoped that someone could deliver them to the family. They later called me and said that the family wanted me to deliver them in person to their new home.

I will never forget that visit, laden with gift wrapped quilts for each of the children. The kids were so excited, they kept hugging and thanking me. The sisters also were very emotional and told me that I was always their favorite nurse and that they never forgot me.

Now that I live thousands of miles away from the islands, I often reminisce and wonder if those kids are still using their quilts, by now thin and ragged, but still filled with my Aloha for the children of Hawaii.

Sunbonnet Sam

*

by **DEBRA MCCLANAHAN**
Coal Valley, Illinois

When I was young, *The Wizard of Oz* was one of my favorite movies. I eagerly awaited the movie being shown on television each year. I was so afraid of the Wicked Witches, but I loved Dorothy, her ruby slippers, and Toto in his basket.

One of the reasons I loved the movie so much was that my grandma was named Dorothy. Her older siblings had L. Frank Baum's story read to them in school and that is why she was named Dorothy.

Grandma enjoyed doing handiwork. She crocheted, quilted, and made a lot of Barbie doll clothes over the years. Grandma and her sister, Aunt Emma, decided to make me a quilt for my 6th birthday as a surprise. Not only did I have my own Dorothy, I also had an Auntie Em! This was way before emails and most people couldn't afford long distance phone calls, so they planned the quilt out through letters because they lived 30 miles apart.

Being a quiet, observant child, I soon found out about the surprise. It was to be a Sunbonnet Sue quilt. I was so excited, but on the big day,

my Sunbonnet Sue was a Sam instead! I asked Grandma why I had gotten a boy quilt and she told me that she and Aunt Emma decided to make it a tomboy quilt because I was such a tomboy. My "Sunbonnet Sam" had solid pink sashing, dainty floral, and pastel plaid overalls, a bucket for gathering blackberries, and he was holding a stick. Why a stick? Dorothy said, "Why that's to scare away snakes when you're out looking for berries!"

What a smart grandma! I loved my quilt and it graced my bed until my college days. As soon as I had my own home, the quilt was on the bed. One thing I could never figure out was why some of the appliqués faced right and the others faced left. I asked Grandma and she told me I would "figure it out someday" and after many years I did.

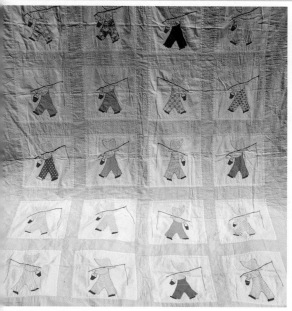

Grandma was right-handed and Aunt Emma was a lefty, so they made the blocks the way that seemed correct to them. What finally helped me make the connection was remembering visiting at Aunt Emma's house and looking at her photo albums. I would sit in the center of the sisters and they would hand the pages to each other. Aunt Emma would sit on my right side and hand off the pages to Grandma on my left. This sitting arrangement must have started when they were young and became a life-long habit.

Now I know which sister made each block and I still sit in the center surrounded by their love. And somewhere over the rainbow, I am sure they are looking at those albums side by side.

Love Never Dies

by **SUSAN CAHILL**
North Tonawanda, NY

When my grandmother turned 90, I made her a special quilt, appliquéd with scenes from her life in Vermont: life on the dairy farm, the school she taught in, the retirement mountain home she and my grandfather built, and the lake front cottage in the North Country. She loved the quilt and used it to illustrate stories she told about her life to her great-grandchildren, letting them sleep under it on special occasions. She lived with my parents and when she fell ill, she would not let the paramedics take her to the hospital until she showed them the quilt. She passed away at 98. Even though I had made special quilts for my parents, Grandma's quilt now was placed on their bed.

One day at work I received a call that my dad had passed away unexpectedly in his sleep at age 71. I was devastated and filled with grief. My husband and I made the eleven-hour trip to my parent's house. My mother told me my dad had been sleeping under the quilt and she had him wrapped in it when he was cremated. Anyone who is not a quilter might find that morbid, but it eased my sorrow to know that

Grandma's quilt made that final journey with him. I felt as if my love was wrapped around him.

The quilt that had touched four generations is now gone from this world, but I believe it lives on. I can picture my father reuniting with my grandparents, wrapping the quilt around them and when my son passed away three years ago, it helped me to know my dad would be there waiting with the quilt. I know that someday I will feel that warmth and comfort too, snuggled under those soft layers with my family.

I believe that love does not die. A quilt can be shared and passed on from one person to another, but the love that goes into the making and giving of a quilt lives on forever for those that give and receive the quilt.

Quilt Therapy

by **JODIANN DONOHUE**
Wyoming, Minnesota

I've been sewing as long as I can remember, but about twenty years ago I decided to take a appliqué class with a friend of mine. We figured it would be a good way to get together since we no longer lived close to each other and I could also stop by to see my grandma and aunt on the way to class.

After a few years, we decided to take a hand piecing class. A few months in I suffered a massive brainstem stroke. It initially took everything but my heartbeat. The doctors told my children that I wouldn't live and if I did, I would be a vegetable. Since God had other plans for me, with the help and prayers of my family and friends, and the work of skilled therapists, I was able to get most of my life back.

After getting home, I fell into a deep depression. Even though I was thankful for my life, I ended up losing my job and my home and moved in with my wonderful daughter and grandson. Since insurance doesn't cover therapy forever, I was trying to figure out what I could do on my own. I ended up getting out my hand sewing project and started working on it again. The stitches were crooked, but my mind could

still figure out how to get my hands and fingers to work. I spent hours sewing each day while watching my grandson Kole play.

I ended up getting a part-time, front desk job at a senior center and they said I could bring my sewing along with me. The people loved it. They would come up to see how far along I was with my project and tell me about their lives and about their family members who also quilted. It was wonderful.

Sewing and quilting have does so much for me. It got me out of that depression, gave me dexterity back in my hands and fingers, helped me connect with people, and gave me confidence and so much more.

Thank you for giving me a chance to share my story.

Our Sewing Room

by **CAROLYN AND CHUCK MILLER**
Kingwood, West Virginia

In 2004, my cousin and I decided we would give quilting a try. We signed up for a beginning quilting class at a local technical school. Once a week we left our husbands at home and scampered off to quilting class. I loved it! Quilting is creative, productive, and relaxing—I was hooked. At first my sewing machine shared my husband's office, yards of gorgeous fabrics, and all my quilting essentials. As I lovingly labored over each project, the satisfaction and enjoyment must have been reflected on my face and my husband took notice.

After a number of years of sharing office space, I decided I needed a little more room and a dedicated location where I could leave quilt projects spread out wherever things happened to be. Thus the idea of a sewing room in our unfinished basement was hatched. Hubby concluded that if I was going to spend all my time in the basement then he wanted to share this new space too. Two rooms connected by a door, which was never closed, were created—one side for my sewing room and one side for his television and jigsaw puzzle room.

Happily, I stacked my stash, plugged in my sewing machine, and worked away on my side of the basement. Periodically, probably during commercials, my spouse would wander over to see what I was up to, ask a question or two, and maybe make a few suggestions. Over time, he began saying he might enjoy quilting as well. When someone gave us some fabric remnants, he was sure he could cut squares and sew them together. And he did! Next was cutting up some of his old flannel shirts to make a raggedy quilt. He was on his way!

Now, several years later, he has a couple of "Best of Show" ribbons from a local festival under his belt, and he makes quilts. Well, I don't need to tell you what happened to those two rooms in the basement. They're still separated by a wall with an open door, but now my side has two sewing machines, one his, one hers, and his side displays his stash and our ironing area. The table, formerly for jigsaw puzzles, now has a large cutting mat.

Most evenings, we gather in our sewing rooms. We talk a little, piece our quilts, and even watch some TV while we work together. It's no longer his room or my room—it's just our two sewing rooms! And we both love quilting!

A Quilt for Pat

✦

by **JEAN MILLER**
Perryville, Missouri

My husband and I volunteer with the United Service Organization (USO) of Missouri. One of our favorite longtime fellow volunteers, Pat, was having a birthday. The leader of our group knew I was a quilter and had saved numerous t-shirts from events and military bases where this volunteer had worked and asked if I could make him a quilt. I agreed, even though I had never made a t-shirt quilt before. I was nervous, but I did my best to make his quilt.

Pat was overwhelmed when it was presented to him. Shortly after that day, we worked an event together and he told me how appreciative he was for the quilt and that he even told his family he wanted to be buried with the quilt. I insisted that he wouldn't have to worry about that for a long time. Pat persisted and later on told me that his family wanted to keep the quilt, but he would have it at his wake.

Suddenly and unbelievably, two months after he had received the quilt, Pat died of a heart attack. When I walked into his wake and saw the t-shirt quilt draped on his casket, my heart melted. I had never felt so honored. It brought tears to my eyes, knowing that quilt meant so much to him.

Pat embodied everything the USO stands for in taking care of our military personnel and their families. He mentored us in our early days of volunteering and became a cherished friend. I am so grateful that I had the opportunity to give something back to him that represented the military groups and bases he held so dear.

I make quilts because I love creating them. My husband said to me one time, "You have no idea how you touch people with your quilts." I had never thought how something I get so much pleasure out of doing could mean so much to others. In Pat's case, it certainly seemed to be true. I hope Pat feels our love, looking down on us, wrapped in a hug and his beloved quilt.

I Used to Have a Baby Quilt

by **DIANNE HOLDER**
Lowgap, North Carolina

Lyla's school teacher contacted me and asked me to bring some of our family quilts to school to show her students at the beginning of the New Year. So my granddaughter and I got out the little red wagon and filled it with some of our favorite quilts. I made sure we brought along some of her baby quilts, especially the "Five Little Monkeys Jumping On the Bed" quilt that she loved so much. We also brought the string quilt that she helped me piece last summer. We even included some strings and a halfway pieced block so she could explain how she made the quilt.

When we arrived at the elementary school, we were greeted by the second grade teachers and they made us feel very welcome. As I entered the classroom, I noticed the twins that Lyla enjoyed playing with so much—a small boy and girl who both sat anxiously on the front row. The twins lived on a family farm right at the base of the Blue Ridge Parkway in a small community. On a cold January morning, the

100-year-old-home that they lived in had caught fire and burned down, destroying all their antiques and family heirlooms.

The children and the teachers seemed to be so interested in what we had inside our little red wagon. They had just finished reading a story about a grandmother who had made a quilt for her granddaughter and talked about what it means to come from a loving and close-knit family.

I let Lyla start our presentation by telling how she had assembled the string quilt. She explained how you could take something as small as two inch fabric strings and smaller pieces of fabric and sew them together to make a quilt top. She explained how to sandwich the batting between the top and backing and quilt the quilt together.

Now, when you are doing a presentation in front of a large group of students, you never know who is listening and who is not paying any attention at all. The children really enjoyed the baby quilts that we passed around for them to hold and feel the cotton fabrics. They seemed to be listening to every word I was saying.

Several small hands were raised. I stopped talking and gave the children a chance to ask questions and tell me about their favorite quilts and who had taken the time to make the family heirlooms in their homes. As we were packing our precious quilts back into the little red wagon, I noticed that David, one of the twins, still had his hand raised. I acknowledged him by saying, "Son do you have a question?" He responded by saying,

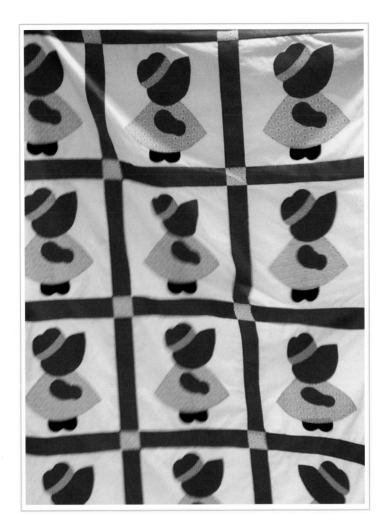

"I have something to tell you." He said that he used to have a baby quilt but he didn't have one anymore. He said that his quilt was destroyed when their house burned down. You could have heard a feather drop in the small classroom. The room was completely silent. I thought my heart would break. I turned toward the teachers to let them say something to take away the very sad moment, but they had turned their backs and were fighting back the tears. What could I say to this small child that would take away the pain that you could see in his pretty brown eyes? All I could think of was saying was, "You know what? I bet that someday, someone who loves you will make your family a new quilt." With a very sheepish grin he responded by saying, "I hope so, but I don't have a grandmother."

After packing up the quilts and leaving the elementary school, I kept hearing the small boy's voice say, "I used to have a baby quilt, but I don't have one anymore." There was only one way to take this hurt away that was deep down in my heart. Just as soon as I entered my home, I got to work in my sewing room. I made the energetic little boy a brand new quilt named "Overhaul Sam." I made his twin sister a beautiful Sunbonnet Sue quilt. I also made their mother and father a rag quilt made out of flannels. I think these quilts will be very fitting for their new country home.

I thank God everyday for my health. I'm so thankful that I have the ability to sew. I am so proud to be a quilter. Each day that I sit at my sewing machine, I have peace in my heart because I can do the things my grandmother taught me to do so many years ago. I pray that my granddaughters will find the same peace in their hearts as they continue to grow up to be wonderful quilters.

Ode to the Rotary Cutter

by **JAN WEBER**
Centennial, Colorado

Your rotary cutter cuts like butter,

But ask me how I know.

It was a Friday 'eve, some stress to relieve,

So quilting here I go.

My ruler was straight, the material flat,

I was ready to cut my first quarter fat.

All of a sudden, that extremely sharp widget,

Had cut the nail off and part of my digit!

So I washed out the wound and took to my bed,

But in the morning my pillow was alarmingly red.

I guess this won't get better without some attention,

So off to the ER was the best intervention.

The doctor had no empathy for my stupidity,

But bandaged me up anyway.

He sent me home with this instruction:

No quilting for the rest of the day.

Take Tylenol for pain and don't get the wound wet,

It will take 3 weeks for your skin to reset.

I could get through some inconvenience and stares,

But how in the world could I wash my long hair?

So spend Friday nights with at least 40 winks,

Quilt on Saturday when you're rested and can think.

Your cutter is your friend and will make quilting fun,

But don't get complacent and give it free run!

*Absolutely no fabric was harmed in the cutting of this finger.

Right on Q

by **SPARKLE DEBO**
Fort Mill, South Carolina

I want to share my craziest quilt story and it's one that no one will ever let me live down! A friend and I designed a quilt for my granddaughter that had appliqué X's and O's all around the border. Each square was a six by six inch square in pink check or white fabric. Alternately, on each square an embroidered four inch appliqué X or O was done. The quilt top was almost complete and I had it hanging on the quilt wall in my bedroom.

One day my young grandson was lying on the bed and I was at the computer. I heard him say, "Grandma, is that quilt for my sister?" and I said "Yes," hardly paying attention. Then he said, "Grandma, why does it have X's and Q's?" I slowly looked over at the quilt, hanging so beautifully in all its glory. Perfectly matched seams, colorful soft pastel blocks with multiple embroidered designs of crowns, fairy tales, cute details, and a border that would show her all the hugs and kisses I wanted to send her way with X's and ... Q's!

For a moment I was dumbfounded and couldn't believe my eyes. Yes, I had made the blocks with Q's instead of O's! This daze lasted only briefly and then my quilting addiction kicked in. I took all the blocks apart and redid the border. The quilt eventually turned out beautifully. My granddaughter was thrilled to get it. And my family ... well you can guess the teasing I still get about the Q's.

Quilting by Phone

by **PAULA CRAMER**
Littleton, Colorado

I have always admired beautiful quilts: large ones, miniature ones, wall hangings, table runners, you name it. If it's quilted, I love it. I have been the recipient of a number of quilts for every season over the years. I have attended a number of quilt shows, purchased many magazines, and even joined a quilt guild so I can admire all the beautiful quilts fellow members share in show and tell. I've even purchased plenty of fabric thinking, "One day I'm going to make a quilt." I've actually bought a few templates, several sewing machines (since I do sewing projects), and pride myself on the stash I have accumulated over the years. But never, not until recently, in my seventieth year, did I attempt to put my tools to work on my own quilt.

It all came about because my daughter lost her pair of French bulldogs when both succumbed to old age within a couple of months of each other. There were many pictures of their adventures over the years. My daughter was absolutely heartbroken. So I decided I might cheer her up a bit, and do so by making her a memory quilt.

Reviewing a number of Internet tutorials and seeing the beautiful fabrics offered and the way quilt making looked to be effortless, I was greatly encouraged. My idea of it being "effortless" changed quickly, however. You know the saying, "You're never too old to learn new things?" Did I ever learn some new things about quilts!

I have a very talented sister who has made a number of quilts over the years, but lives about 1,400 miles from me, so I rang her up and told her of my decision. We decided to, literally, quilt by phone. I don't know if you have ever made a quilt by phone. It is an exciting but challenging task. When one lacks self-confidence for such an undertaking, it helps to call on a talented friend or clever family member to bolster your confidence and then, plunge on ahead. My sister did just that for me. "You can do this," and "Just be patient" were her most endearing comments. Every time there was a question or I got stumped on a technique, I sent a text, called her on the phone, or sent a photo with my cell.

After one telephone conversation after another about color, shapes, patterns, pictures, printing, cutting, and seam allowances, my quilt actually began to take shape! I'm convinced had I not had unlimited minutes and data on my cell phone, I could have made a dent in the national debt to pay for calls and photos sent back and forth to show progress and accomplishment. So our "telephone quilting bee" time added up, first to minutes, then hours, and, ultimately, days.

Many a time over the weeks, I made the plunge to do something as simple as pressing the seams on the quilt top open before a call to my sister, only to get the instruction that seams are not pressed open, as in regular sewing projects, and a valuable time-consuming lesson was learned.

At last, the day came. I put the label on the back of my quilt, wrapped the treasure up, and dropped the package in the mail. There was such a feeling of exuberance and great satisfaction to know that, yes, I can make a quilt. It may not be as perfect as a quilt showpiece, but a lot of hard work and dedication was in that package. When the phone rang and my daughter began expressing her joy at such a beautiful and cherished quilt made by her mom, well then all that time, effort, and fun spent with my sister over the phone was so worth it. And you know what? I'm gonna make another quilt.